Original title:
Frozen Moose

Copyright © 2024 Swan Charm

Author: Linda Leevike
ISBN HARDBACK: 978-9908-52-350-7
ISBN PAPERBACK: 978-9908-52-351-4
ISBN EBOOK: 978-9908-52-352-1

Glacial Echoes

Whispers dance on icy air,
Sparkling lights without a care.
Chill of laughter fills the night,
Hearts aglow in festive light.

Snowflakes twirl, a joyful flight,
Warming fires, the pure delight.
Glacial echoes ring so clear,
Bringing friends and festive cheer.

The Silhouette in Frost

Shadows play on crystals bright,
Silver glimmers in the light.
Trees adorned with frosted lace,
Nature's hush, a soft embrace.

Children's voices fill the air,
Joyful moments everywhere.
Sipping cocoa, hearts entwined,
In this scene, pure peace we find.

Nature's Stillness

Silent nights with stars aglow,
Moonlight dances on the snow.
Branches bow with starlit grace,
Nature holds a warm embrace.

Fires crackle, stories shared,
In the stillness, hearts are bared.
Gather close, let worries cease,
In this calm, we find our peace.

Hooves in the Winter Mist

Hooves a-patter on the ground,
Magic whispers all around.
Wrapped in blankets, snug and tight,
We cheer the beauty of the night.

Sleigh bells jingle through the air,
Every moment filled with care.
Through the mist, we ride anew,
In this wonder, all feels true.

Nature's Giant in Stillness

In the forest, whispers glide,
Tall trees stand, their secrets hide.
Golden leaves like sunlit dreams,
Nature's heart in quiet gleams.

Birds chirp sweet in morning light,
Colors dance, a pure delight.
Under skies of azure blue,
Life unfolds in vibrant hue.

Hooves Print Stories in Snow

Hooves press gently on the white,
Tales of journeys day and night.
Frosty air where laughter swirls,
Winter's joy unfurls and twirls.

Each print tells of paths once roamed,
In the wild where spirits called home.
Snowflakes fall like whispered charms,
Nature's grace in soft, warm arms.

Timeless Beauty of the North

Underneath the starry dome,
Glaciers gleam where wild things roam.
Mountains rise, their peaks so high,
Kissed by clouds that float like sighs.

Auroras dance in vibrant hues,
A canvas bright with nature's muse.
In the stillness, peace unfolds,
Timeless tales, forever told.

Crystalized Dreams of the Wild

In the twilight, magic glows,
Every heartbeat gently flows.
Crystals form where rivers bend,
Nature's art, our hearts it sends.

Footprints mark the path of grace,
In this wild and wondrous space.
Underneath the moon's soft light,
Dreams take flight in tranquil night.

Beneath the Whispering Snow

Flakes twirl gently in the light,
They dance and laugh in pure delight.
Children's laughter fills the air,
Joy abounds everywhere.

Warmth in hearts, a glowing fire,
Songs sung loud, our spirits higher.
Mittens clasped, we run and play,
Chasing dreams on winter's day.

The Stillness of a Forgotten Trail

Crimson leaves beneath white sheen,
Silent whispers where we've been.
Footprints traced in crisp, cool air,
Nature's art beyond compare.

The scent of pine, a tranquil grace,
Winding paths in this serene place.
Snowflakes shimmer, a soft embrace,
Time stands still, a sweet space.

Encased in Winter's Embrace

Icicles glisten, diamonds bright,
Underneath the silver light.
Every corner, a wonder found,
Magic in this frosty ground.

Families gather, warm and tight,
Sharing stories through the night.
Hot cocoa spills, marshmallows float,
Joyful hearts and laughter wrote.

Life Within the Icebound Realm

Beneath the frost, the world sleeps deep,
Winter whispers, secrets keep.
Creatures stir, the air is still,
Nature's heart beats, quiet thrill.

Stars above in a velvet sky,
Glistening dreams as time slips by.
In the chill, the warmth we sow,
Together, we thrive beneath the snow.

Silent Steps in Snow

Softly fall the flakes today,
Children laugh and dance and play,
Footprints trace a merry path,
In the chill, we share our laugh.

Warmth of cocoa, sweet delight,
Glowing candles, spirits bright,
Winter's charm, a family cheer,
Holding close those we hold dear.

Snowflakes twirl like wishes free,
In this land of purity,
Every step, a joyful song,
Together here, we all belong.

A Shimmer of Frost

Morning light brings crystal gleam,
Nature glows, a wondrous dream,
Frosty branches, silver trails,
Whispers of the season's tales.

Laughter echoes in the air,
Joyful hearts, we've come to share,
Sipping warm and spicy treats,
Gathered where the friendship meets.

Every twinkle, every glow,
Brings us closer, love to grow,
In this festive, frosty bliss,
Moments like this, we'll not miss.

The Stillness of the Wild

In the woods, a blanket white,
Nature sleeps, yet feels so bright,
Animals hide, a secret blend,
In this peace, we find a friend.

Stars above, a canopy,
Silent night, serenity,
Footsteps crunch on snowy ground,
In the stillness, magic found.

Snowflakes dance in winter's breath,
Whispers soft, a voice from death,
Life renews, despite the cold,
In the wild, great tales unfold.

Whispers Beneath the Snow

Beneath the blanket, life sleeps low,
Dreams are woven in the snow,
Every flake, a story told,
Of warmth and joy, in binding hold.

Frosty air, a gentle kiss,
Hearts ignite in winter's bliss,
Crisp and clear, the twilight glows,
In the hush, the magic flows.

Gather 'round, the fire's light,
Filling souls with pure delight,
Voices rise in harmony,
In this season, wild and free.

Permafrost Portraits

In the gleam of winter's light,
Colors dance, a dazzling sight.
Joyful hearts on snowy trails,
Whispers of laughter fill the gales.

Carved in ice, a fleeting state,
Frozen gems that celebrate.
Children's voices fill the air,
Festive echoes everywhere.

Crisp and bright, the world adorned,
Hot cocoa cups, warm hands warmed.
Lighting fires that softly glow,
Permafrost, art in frozen flow.

Silence in the Snow

Blanket white, the earth does wear,
In the stillness, magic's flair.
Footsteps quiet on the ground,
In this hush, pure peace is found.

Glistening flakes in swirling play,
As the world, in dreams, does sway.
Joyful songs of winter's hue,
In the silence, thoughts anew.

Candles flicker, warm and bright,
Ember glow on wintry night.
Celebration in the cold,
Memories of warmth retold.

Emblems of the Cold

Icicles hang like crystal spears,
Marking moments, frozen years.
Festive lights on branches sway,
Painting nights in bright array.

Frosty breath in the evening air,
Stars above like gems laid bare.
Winter's charm, a wondrous sight,
Joy and laughter take their flight.

Gathered near the flame we share,
Stories dance, a festive flare.
Emblems etched in frost so fine,
Each moment, magical, divine.

Paws Upon the Frozen Ground

Tracks of joy, a playful sound,
Paws upon the frozen ground.
Little friends, in white they frolic,
Winter's fun, pure and symbolic.

Chasing snowflakes, wild and free,
Boundless spirits, unity.
In the chill, their laughter blooms,
As the world in joy resumes.

Firelight dances, warm embrace,
In our hearts, a festive space.
Paws imprint the frosty scene,
Winter whispers, soft and keen.

Glacial Guardian of the Forest

Under the shimmering trees, they stand,
Whispers of magic drift through the land.
Snowflakes dance in the crisp, bright air,
Joyful laughter echoes, a song so rare.

Icicles glisten in the warm sun's light,
Nature's wonders, a pure delight.
Frosted branches, like lace, they gleam,
In this winter wonderland, we dream.

Creatures stir, dressed in coats of white,
Hearts are lifted, spirits take flight.
Gather together, friends hand in hand,
In the embrace of this enchanted land.

Celebrate with cheer, let warmth ignite,
A glacial guardian, a magical sight.
With each step, we cherish the scene,
A festive memory, forever serene.

Winter's Silent Monolith

In the heart of the woods, so still and grand,
A monolith rises, a frosted stand.
Whispers of silence fill the cool night air,
Beneath the moon's glow, nothing can compare.

Stars twinkle brightly in the velvet sky,
While snowflakes flutter gently on by.
Hushed breaths surround, like a soft embrace,
In this winter realm, time slows its pace.

Embers of joy spark in every heart,
As we gather close, never to part.
Hot cocoa steams, a welcoming cheer,
In the warmth of our love, the chill disappears.

A celebration born from heart and soul,
As we dance 'round the fire, we feel whole.
Winter's monolith, a sentinel bright,
Guiding us through this magical night.

Shadows of the Frostbitten Woods

In shadows deep where the frostbite clings,
Whispers of wonder and the joy it brings.
Footprints in snow lead to secrets untold,
As magic unfolds in the silent cold.

Twinkling lights soften the dark's embrace,
Laughter and warmth create a sacred space.
Gathered together, we share stories old,
In the heart of the woods, our memories unfold.

Each branch heavy-laden with snow's gentle kiss,
Wrapped in enchantment, we find our bliss.
The chill in the air is a thrill to our hearts,
In this festive dance, the spirit imparts.

Songs of the season fill the chilly night,
Shadows of joy bring the world pure light.
United we stand, in frosted delight,
Embracing the beauty of winter's white might.

Serenity Wrapped in White

The world lies blanketed in soft, pure white,
A tranquil moment, a heartwarming sight.
Frost-kissed branches sway in the breeze,
As laughter rings out through the dancing trees.

Families gather around the warm flame,
Exchanging good wishes, joy is the aim.
With each joyful glance, we share the delight,
In a season of laughter, shining so bright.

Snowmen arise with eyes made of stone,
Each crafted with love, a smile widely shown.
Children at play, their hearts so light,
Creating fond memories in the sparkling night.

In serenity wrapped, we find pure cheer,
United in joy that we hold dear.
The spirit of winter dances, embraces us tight,
In this blissful moment, everything feels right.

Glacial Graces

Ice crystals twirl in swirling light,
Snowflakes dance, oh what a sight!
Children laugh with cheer and glee,
Nature's charm, wild and free.

Fires crackle, warmth surrounds,
Joyful noise in playful sounds.
A glow, a shimmer, a festive air,
Hearts are light, gathered with care.

Twinkling lights on frosty greens,
Magic woven in sparkling scenes.
Gifts exchanged with love and grace,
Moments cherished, time to embrace.

Let us toast to frosty nights,
Filled with laughter, love, and sights.
With glacial graces, we unite,
In this wonderland, pure delight.

Shadows in a Winter's Tale

Beneath the moon, in frosty glow,
Whispers weave where cold winds blow.
Shadows dance on Christmas eve,
In dreams of warmth, we all believe.

Pine trees clad in snowy veils,
Echoes of laughter paint the trails.
Hot cocoa sipped in cozy nooks,
Stories shared from treasured books.

Carols sung with purest voice,
In every heart, a chance to rejoice.
Stars above, they brightly gleam,
In winter's tale, we share a dream.

Fireside chats, a soothing sound,
Magic of the night unbound.
Together we find peace and cheer,
Shadows whisper, winter near.

Frigid Dreams of a Stately Beast

In the heart of the frozen wood,
Where silence reigns, and time has stood.
A stately beast roams, brave and bold,
Frigid dreams in its heart, untold.

Snowflakes kiss its mighty back,
Soft and gentle on the track.
In this realm, of white and blue,
Magic flows in every view.

Hushed whispers of the night sky,
As a chill breeze dances by.
The world asleep in softest peace,
But in its dreams, the magic won't cease.

For every breath, a cloud of mist,
The beast knows love in winter's tryst.
Through glades adorned in purest grace,
In frosty dreams, a warm embrace.

Crystal Kingdoms

Welcome to realms where the cold winds sigh,
Crystal kingdoms beneath the sky.
Icicles shimmer as sunbeams play,
In this winter wonder, we find our way.

Fields of white, so vast and wide,
With laughter echoing side by side.
Joyful hearts in a festive fold,
In the embrace of winter's hold.

Sleigh bells ringing, the night alive,
In crystal dreams, we come to thrive.
A journey sweet, where spirits climb,
Together we make the best of time.

From frosty trees our wishes flow,
As we dance in the radiant glow.
In crystal kingdoms, we shall play,
A festive spirit, come what may.

Chilled Antlers in the Mist

In the meadow where the snowflakes dance,
Chilled antlers rise in a silvery trance.
The mist wraps around like a soft embrace,
Nature's wonders fill this frozen space.

Laughter echoes in the crisp, cold air,
Joyful gatherings, friendships laid bare.
With mugs of cocoa, we share our dreams,
Under starlit skies and bright moonbeams.

Crimson scarves and cheerful hats,
Spinning circles with our playful spats.
Each twirl releases a flurry of white,
In this festive moment, hearts feel so light.

As we toast to the magic of this night,
Chilled antlers glimmer, a beautiful sight.
With every breath, the sparkles ignite,
In the mist of this winter, everything feels right.

Silent Steps on Ice

Silent steps on a glimmering lake,
Where the world sleeps, a calm we partake.
The moonlight twinkles on the frozen ground,
In this peaceful scene, happiness found.

Skates glide softly with a whispering sound,
Around the rink, joyfulness abound.
Warming spirits with laughter and cheer,
As friends come together, the season is near.

Snowflakes swirl in a grand ballet,
While fireside stories keep the cold at bay.
With each gentle glide, memories are spun,
Silent steps on ice, where hearts become one.

In this winter wonder, we celebrate all,
Together we rise, together we fall.
Bathed in starlight, the night feels divine,
With silent steps on ice, our spirits align.

The Arctic Sentinel

In the land where the northern lights play,
The Arctic sentinel stands tall, ablaze.
A guardian of frost, in beauty it reigns,
Binding the magic of winter's domains.

With a cloak of snow, so pure and so bright,
It watches over through the long, dark night.
Icicles shimmer like chandeliers grand,
Reflecting the joy of this frozen land.

Gathered around with hearts full of cheer,
With stories of warmth, we hold each other near.
The air is electric, our laughter rings clear,
In the embrace of the sentinel, we feel no fear.

Each star above twinkles in delight,
While shadows dance softly in the silver light.
The Arctic sentinel, a festive embrace,
In the heart of winter, we find our place.

Whispering Pines and Frosted Dreams

Under whispering pines, where magic is spun,
Frosted dreams twinkle, a dream to be won.
Wrapped in cold magic, beneath winter's glance,
The world holds its breath in a sparkling dance.

Candles flicker, their glow warm and bright,
Guiding us gently through the long, dark night.
With each shared story, the bonds start to grow,
In festive moments, our hearts feel the glow.

Snow-laden branches, a canvas so white,
Sparkling like treasures in the soft, silver light.
We carve laughter and joy into the air,
With every connection, the warmth we share.

As dreams unfold in the frosted expanse,
We cherish the moments, we cherish each chance.
Under whispering pines, together we'll gleam,
In this winter wonder, we chase every dream.

Glint of the Frozen Realm

In the frost-kissed air, laughter sings,
Dancing snowflakes on shimmering wings.
Children's joy in the crisp, bright light,
Surrounded by magic, hearts take flight.

Sparkling crystals on branches gleam,
Whispers of wonder in every dream.
The world transformed, a canvas fair,
A festive haven in the winter air.

The Snow-Cloaked Guardian

Beneath the cloak of soft, white snow,
The guardian watches, silent and slow.
With every flake that kisses the ground,
A timeless magic in silence is found.

Lights twinkle bright in the deepening night,
Joyful voices carry, hearts feel light.
In this wondrous world wrapped tight and warm,
The snow-cloaked guardian keeps us from harm.

Glimmering in the Twilight

As twilight falls, the stars emerge,
Frosty air holds a gentle urge.
To gather 'round the fire's embrace,
And share in laughter, a joyful space.

The glimmering night in vibrant hues,
Every twinkling light brings the muse.
With stories spun and memories shared,
In the magic of twilight, hearts prepared.

Mirrors of the Icy Grove

In the grove where the ice does gleam,
Mirrors of frost reflect each dream.
Branches adorned with delicate lace,
Nature's beauty in this sacred place.

As festive spirits twirl and play,
Under the moon's soft, silvery sway.
The whispers of winter, sweet and clear,
In the icy grove, we hold dear.

Reflections in a Frozen Stream

Beneath the ice, the colors blend,
A shimmering dance, where daylight bends.
The sun's bright rays, like sparkling gems,
In frozen pools, nature's diadems.

Children gather, laughter fills the air,
Joyful shouts, as snowflakes swirl fair.
With each bold leap, the world seems bright,
In winter's grasp, hearts take flight.

The trees adorned in white's soft lace,
A wondrous sight, a lovely embrace.
Twinkling lights, in every nook,
As the stream flows on, a winter book.

Reflections dance, a fleeting glance,
In this frozen world, let's take a chance.
Together we'll roam, through time and space,
In the joy of now, we find our place.

A Whisper of Nature's Breath

The frost-kissed morn, a gentle sigh,
Nature awakes, as dreams float by.
A whisper soft, on crisp, cold air,
Invites the heart to wander, to care.

The pines wear coats of powdered white,
While laughter echoes, pure delight.
Children chase the snowflakes' flight,
Under the glow of winter's light.

With mugs of cocoa, warm and bright,
We gather close, hearts feeling light.
Stories shared in flickering fire,
Igniting sense of sweet desire.

A tranquil hush, as stars emerge,
In this frozen realm, we gently surge.
Together we breathe, the winter's song,
In nature's arms, where we belong.

Cold Silence

In the stillness, a chill descends,
Whispers of snow where quiet tends.
A world asleep, wrapped up in white,
With beauty cloaked, in soft twilight.

Footsteps muffled, a gentle tread,
Each flake a tale, in silence spread.
Branches bowed with a heavy load,
As winter weaves its silent road.

The air is crisp, a breath divine,
In frozen time, all hearts align.
Together we stand, beneath the skies,
In this cold stillness, time flies.

Nature awaits, our laughter weaves,
In wondrous peace, a heart that believes.
We dance in shadows, with dreams to dream,
In the cherished tales of cold silence, we gleam.

The Frozen Figure

A silhouette stands amidst the snow,
In winter's grasp, a tale to bestow.
With arms outstretched, in purest grace,
The frozen figure, a timeless space.

Through swirling winds, it holds its ground,
Where echoes of cheer are truly found.
In laughter loud, and voices clear,
It captures joy, it holds us near.

The canvas white, with colors bright,
With every motion, we take flight.
Against the chill, our spirits soar,
In this frozen dance, we ask for more.

As dusk descends, the stars ignite,
In winter's embrace, our hearts take flight.
Together we write, in magical ink,
The frozen figure, our hearts in sync.

The Icy Majesty Unfurling

In the glow of the crisp cold night,
Icicles dance, shimmering bright.
The stars adorn the velvet sky,
Whispers of joy as the snowflakes fly.

Gathered around the fire's warm embrace,
Laughter echoes in this magical space.
Hot cocoa swirls in cups held high,
Toasting to dreams and moments that sigh.

Festive lights twinkle on every tree,
A chorus of love sings wild and free.
Wrapped in warmth, spirits ignite,
This icy majesty feels just right.

Together we twirl, hearts in a whirl,
As winter's wonders unfurl and unfurl.
In the charm of this night, we shall find,
The magic of joy, forever entwined.

Solitude in the Winter Woods

Softly falling, the snow takes flight,
Blanketing the woods in a veil of white.
Footsteps crunch on the frozen ground,
In the stillness, peace is found.

Tall pines wear their frosty crown,
While silence wraps the world in a gown.
A solitary bird begins to sing,
Celebrating the gifts that winter brings.

Hushed whispers of wind through branches sway,
Echoes of dreams where the heart shall play.
Frost-kissed beauty, a sight to behold,
Nurturing warmth in the bitter cold.

In this solitude, a festive mirth,
A moment to cherish, a treasure of worth.
For in winter's quiet, we rediscover,
The magic that lies in the heart of the other.

The Still Heart of December

December's chill wraps the day,
As lanterns flicker, guiding our way.
Frosty breath dances in the air,
Gathered with friends, laughter we share.

Stories ignite like the fire's warm glow,
Tales of the year and the seeds we'll sow.
Under stars that twinkle and gleam,
Together we weave the fabric of dream.

Cinnamon spices and cookies abound,
A sweet celebration in love's soft sound.
As snowflakes pirouette on a winter breeze,
We wrap our hearts in moments like these.

In the stillness, joy takes the lead,
The magic we seek is in every seed.
With each heartbeat, December unfolds,
A story of warmth as the year turns bold.

The Silent Whisper of Cold

Snowflakes dance upon the breeze,
Gentle whispers from the trees.
Laughter echoes, joy and cheer,
In the stillness, warmth draws near.

Candles glow with golden light,
Filling hearts on this cold night.
Friends gather, stories unfold,
In the magic of the cold.

Gifts wrapped up in ribbons bright,
Every moment feels just right.
The world becomes a wondrous place,
With winter's soft and sweet embrace.

Dreams in Winter's Chill

Under the stars, the snow does gleam,
Blanketing dreams in a silvery beam.
Children play, their spirits soar,
Winter's joy we all adore.

Hot cocoa brews, the fireplace glows,
Every heart feels love that grows.
Cozy blankets, laughter shared,
In the chill, we are all cared.

Twinkling lights, a festive sight,
Gathered close, hearts feel so light.
In winter's breath, we find our thrill,
Within the magic of winter's chill.

A Tapestry of Ice

Icicles hang like crystal dreams,
Nature's art, or so it seems.
Each shimmer tells a tale of old,
A tapestry of ice and gold.

Lively snowmen dot the park,
Their scarves bright against the dark.
Children's laughter fills the air,
In these moments, joy we share.

Fires crackle, hearts grow warm,
Amid the winter's chilly charm.
Time slows down, we breathe it in,
This festive vibe, where smiles begin.

Beautifully Bound in White

A quilt of snow wraps the ground,
In its hush, no other sound.
Trees adorned in winter's lace,
Each branch holds a proud embrace.

Families gather, spirits bright,
Underneath the starry night.
Songs of joy fill every heart,
As we share, we play our part.

With every twinkle, every cheer,
Moments cherished, held so dear.
Beautifully bound, this scene so right,
We celebrate in pure delight.

The Hidden Heart Beneath the Snow

Beneath the white, a pulse of cheer,
Soft whispers of life, they draw near.
Joy dances in flakes, twirls in the air,
A secret warmth, everywhere.

Laughter spills forth from every tree,
Branches cloaked in purest glee.
In frost-kissed light, the world aglow,
Revealing the heart beneath the snow.

Candles flicker, casting a glow,
As stars above begin to show.
Together we celebrate, hand in hand,
The hidden heart in this winter land.

An Elegy for Lost Warmth

When the fire fades, shadows creep,
Echoes of laughter, memories we keep.
Winter's chill wraps us tight,
Yet hope blooms soft in the night.

With each breath, the frost does sing,
Whispers of warmth the season brings.
Though the hearth feels cold and alone,
Passion ignites in the heart's tone.

Gather close in this wintry plight,
Share stories that shimmer in candlelight.
For every loss, there's joy to create,
An elegy whispered, yet never too late.

Midnight in the Frozen Glade

At midnight's stroke, the world stands still,
A blanket of snow o'er every hill.
In the frozen glade, a hush profound,
The magic of winter, all around.

Stars twinkle bright in the velvet sky,
A serenade for the soft snowflakes' sigh.
Shadows dance 'neath the moonlit glow,
In this tranquil realm, spirits flow.

Hearts entwined in the peaceful night,
Warmth whispers softly in the cold moonlight.
Together we bask in this winter's reign,
In a frozen glade, love shall remain.

The Enigma of a Winter Wanderer

Through snowy paths, the wanderer roams,
In each footprint, the mystery combs.
Glistening trails in a silent town,
Where laughter's echo wears a gown.

With eyes aglow, they search the night,
For fleeting warmth, for a spark of light.
Every corner holds a story untold,
In the arms of winter, brave and bold.

Snowflakes twirl like dreams in flight,
Guided by stars, shimmering bright.
A heart beats strong, a spirit so free,
In the enigma of winter, joy will be.

Beneath the Layered Silence

Snowflakes dance with gentle grace,
Whispers of cheer in every place.
Children laugh, their voices rise,
Underneath the winter skies.

Candles glow with warmth so bright,
Hearts aglow in the soft twilight.
Families gather, stories shared,
Love's embrace, a gift declared.

Carols sung in joyful tones,
Fires crackle, comfort known.
Hope is wrapped in festive cheer,
Beneath the silence, joy is near.

Mirthful sighs, the night unveiled,
With every heart, the season hailed.
Together we find our delight,
Beneath the layered silent night.

Shimmering Shadows in Winter Light

Twinkling lights through branches gleam,
Casting warmth, igniting dreams.
Frosted windows, secrets keep,
While snowflakes over the sidewalks leap.

A gentle breeze makes spirits soar,
With laughter echoing evermore.
In every home, a festive glow,
As shimmering shadows softly flow.

Mittens worn, hands intertwined,
In winter's magic, hearts aligned.
Drinks in hand, we toast the night,
In the shimmer, all feels right.

Moments cherished, traditions reign,
Creating joy from every strain.
In winter's light, let spirits bright
Guide us through this lovely night.

Echoes of a Winter Stroll

Footprints pressed in powdery white,
Echo through the starry night.
Whispers carried on the air,
Winter's song, a breath so rare.

Glistening paths with ice enshrined,
With every step, warmth intertwined.
Laughter dances, hearts unite,
In the joy of the chilly night.

Bonfires burn with crackling cheer,
Neighbors gather, loved ones near.
Stories shared like treasured gold,
In winter's grasp, we're gently bold.

Every echo, a memory made,
In winter's charm, we can't evade.
So let's embrace this lovely stroll,
As the winter night warms the soul.

Frosted Majesty Unveiled

Glistening landscapes, pure and bright,
Frosted beauty, a charming sight.
Trees adorned in sparkling lace,
Nature's art, a grand embrace.

Joyful voices, cheer abounds,
Making magic, spinning rounds.
In this wonder, hearts entwine,
Frosted moments termed divine.

Candied treats and laughter sweet,
Gather 'round, where friends will meet.
Gifts of love, with ribbons tied,
In frosted majesty, we take pride.

Winter's chill brings warmth inside,
With joyous mirth, we will abide.
Let hearts celebrate and prevail,
As frost unveils a festive tale.

The Solitary Wanderer

Through twinkling lights and shadows found,
A wanderer drifts on festive ground.
Each step a beat, a heart so free,
In city squares, where joy flies free.

With laughter ringing, souls unite,
While whispers dance with pure delight.
The moon above, a silver cheer,
Guides every dream, dispels all fear.

In solitude, yet thrumming bright,
He finds his peace in starry night.
The world a canvas, colors swirl,
A festive song, the dreams unfurl.

So let the journey weave its tale,
In every rhythm, leaving a trail.
The wanderer smiles with every stride,
For in this cheer, he'll always bide.

Imprints in the Powdered White

In fields of white, the laughter flows,
Where every step a memory sows.
Snowflakes dance in winter's grace,
A joyous time, a warm embrace.

Children's footprints, a playful march,
Underneath the bright arch.
Each snowball thrown, a delight to see,
Echoes of glee, wild and free.

The air is crisp, the sky so clear,
By fireside tales, we gather near.
Around the tree, with love we twine,
Imprints of joy, in hearts they shine.

Every flake a story told,
In winter's grasp, we are bold.
Together we stand, no one alone,
In powdered white, our love has grown.

A Glacial Lullaby

In icy realms, where dreams take flight,
The glacial breath sings through the night.
Softly it whispers, a gentle tune,
Beneath the spell of a winter moon.

The stars twinkle like distant chimes,
As snowflakes weave through whispered rhymes.
A lullaby drapes the world in white,
Embracing magic, pure and bright.

With every chill, warm hearts ignite,
For warmth is found in shared delight.
In frosted air, our laughter glides,
A symphony of joy abides.

So let the night wrap us so tight,
With glacial dreams, our spirits light.
Through every note, our hopes arise,
A lullaby beneath the skies.

Frosty Reverie

Upon the ground, a crystalline gleam,
The frost weaves magic, like a dream.
Nature's artistry, bold and bright,
Transforming day to wondrous night.

In every breath, a spark of cheer,
Whispers of warmth, the season near.
With cocoa sips and laughter shared,
In frosty reverie, none are scared.

The world adorned in silver coats,
As joy floats in, on gentle boats.
Together we dance in rhythmic grace,
Finding our hope in winter's embrace.

So raise a glass, let spirits soar,
In frosty cheer, forevermore.
With every smile, our hearts entwine,
Embracing joy, in frost divine.

Shadows on the Glaciers

Beneath the bright auroras so clear,
Dancing shadows bring festive cheer.
Icicles glitter in the moon's soft glow,
Whispers of winter in delicate flow.

Laughter echoes through frosty air,
Joyful spirits, a celebration laid bare.
The world adorned in a blanket of white,
Hearts are merry on this long winter night.

Children's laughter and footsteps alike,
Tracing paths where the old trees strike.
Mirthful gatherings, stories retold,
As warmth unfolds in the evening's cold.

Together we cherish these moments so bright,
Shadows dancing, a beautiful sight.
In the stillness, our fancies take flight,
Under the stars, we bask in the night.

Whispers of the Untamed

In forests where wild creatures play,
Nature's music invites us to stay.
Lively colors paint the scene,
A festival echoing wild and serene.

Leaves twirl down in a vibrant embrace,
The spirit of nature, a joyful trace.
Every rustle brings laughter anew,
Whispers and giggles beneath skies so blue.

Bubbles of laughter float on the breeze,
Crisp and clear like the shimmering trees.
Footsteps dance over soft, mossy ground,
In this wild wonder, happiness found.

As dusk draws near and stars start to glow,
We gather together beneath snowflakes aglow.
Fireside tales roll into the night,
In the heart of the wild, all feels just right.

The Winter's Embrace

Branches bow low in the gentle frost,
Nature's beauty, a treasure embossed.
Flakes like diamonds fall from the sky,
In winter's embrace, we breathe and sigh.

Warmth spills from fires, a radiant glow,
A circle of friends where warm drinks flow.
Songs of the season fill the chilly air,
Bonded together, we show that we care.

Candles flicker, casting soft light,
The chill outside can't dampen our night.
Wrapped in blankets, we share our tales,
Of love and laughter on soft, snowy trails.

Embracing the season with hearts open wide,
In the winter's hug, we shall abide.
A tapestry woven with all the delight,
In the stillness of snow, our spirits take flight.

A Dance of Ice and Snow

Crystal ornaments twinkle like stars,
A dance of ice beneath the night's bars.
Footsteps glide on the frozen lake,
In swirling snowflakes, dreams awake.

Bonfires crackle with warmth and glow,
Gathered around, we savor the show.
Friends together in chilly delight,
Sharing stories that warm the night.

The world outside wrapped in silver threads,
A place where joy through whispers spreads.
Raindrops of snow sprinkle cheer from above,
In nature's embrace, we feel the love.

As the night deepens, the music flows free,
Hearts intertwined in winter's decree.
We dance and rejoice beneath the moon's shine,
In a festival of ice where our spirits align.

Shapes in the Icy Landscape

Sparkling snowflakes drift and spin,
Creating shapes where dreams begin.
Laughter echoes in crisp, cold air,
Joyful hearts dance without a care.

Twinkling lights brighten the night,
Frosted branches, a wondrous sight.
Children build their snowmen tall,
In this magical land, we find it all.

Every corner, a story told,
Winter's charm, a sight to behold.
With sleds that glide down hills of white,
The world transformed in pure delight.

So let us raise a cheer for snow,
In the icy landscape, let love flow.
Together we celebrate and play,
In this festive scene, let's seize the day.

Nature's Frozen Sentinel

Glistening trees stand proud and tall,
Guardians of winter, watching all.
Whispers of snowflakes softly fall,
Nature's beauty, a sweet enthrall.

The air is crisp, the world aglow,
In this serene kingdom, spirits grow.
Frost-kissed petals, a delicate sight,
Infuse our hearts with festive light.

Beneath the stars, the moon will beam,
Lighting our path, igniting dreams.
A chill in the air, yet warmth we find,
In every heartbeat, love intertwined.

Come gather 'round, let voices rise,
In nature's embrace, where laughter flies.
Together we share this chilly cheer,
Nature's sentinel keeps us near.

The Chilling Grace

Winter's breath, a gentle sigh,
Snowflakes tumble through the sky.
They dance and twirl in frosty grace,
A festive waltz, a bright embrace.

Each flake unique, a story spun,
In the land where the chill has begun.
Hot cocoa shared by a crackling fire,
In this season, our spirits aspire.

Crimson and gold adorn the trees,
Echoes of joy ride on the breeze.
With friends beside and laughter near,
The chilling grace brings us cheer.

Through the night, we embrace the glow,
As stars above shine soft and low.
Together we weave memories fine,
In winter's tapestry, hearts align.

A Dance With Winter's Spirit

The spirit of winter invites us near,
To join in a dance filled with cheer.
With every twirl, we laugh and play,
In this frosty tableau, joy on display.

Footprints trail in the soft, white snow,
As colorful scarves in the wind flow.
The world transforms in this sparkling light,
A festival of dreams, a wondrous sight.

Let's spin and glide under the moon,
In harmony with winter's tune.
Where snowflakes whisper sweet refrain,
In the embrace of the cold, we gain.

So take my hand, let's weave and sway,
As winter's spirit guides our way.
In this endless dance, our hearts ignite,
Together, we shine in the starry night.

Echoes of a Winter World

Snowflakes dance in chilly air,
Laughter echoes everywhere.
Lights aglow on every street,
Joy and warmth in every heartbeat.

Children building forts of white,
Mittens snug, the world feels right.
Carols sung with voices bright,
Winter's magic, pure delight.

The hearth aflame, the kettle sings,
In this season, love takes wings.
Gather close, let stories flow,
In the warmth, our spirits grow.

In the quiet, wonders shine,
Embracing all, a sacred sign.
Echoes of a world adorned,
In winter's arms, we are reborn.

The Iced Pathwalker

Through frosty trees, a path does gleam,
Footprints whisper in a dream.
Glittering snow beneath each tread,
Where adventure and wonder spread.

The air is crisp, the silence deep,
Nature's beauty, ours to keep.
Each step forward, a tale unfolds,
In winter's grasp, adventure holds.

A hidden world beneath the frost,
Where laughter lives, and worries lost.
Walk with me, where spirits soar,
On this icy path, forevermore.

With hearts aglow, we wander wide,
In the magic, world beside.
Together here, our dreams ignite,
In the wonder of winter's light.

Frost's Countenance

Beneath the stars, the frost does gleam,
A tapestry woven from a dream.
Each crystal sparkles in the night,
Nature's canvas, pure and bright.

With every breath, the cold ignites,
Wrapped in warmth, we chase the lights.
Laughter shares the winter's song,
In this festivity, we belong.

Around the fire, tales unfold,
Of ancient whispers, brave and bold.
In the glow, connections made,
In the warmth of hearts displayed.

A gathering of souls so dear,
In frost's countenance, we cheer.
Together we embrace the night,
In winter's charm, we find our light.

The Enchanted Winter Path

Along the trail, the lanterns glow,
Casting shadows in the snow.
Whispers of enchantment rise,
Beneath the dark, a world of skies.

With every step, a story near,
As laughter dances, hearts feel clear.
A snowball fight, a joyful cheer,
In this moment, we are here.

The scent of pine, the frost in air,
Wrapped together, without a care.
Each breath a promise, pure and true,
In our hearts, the magic grew.

As moonlight spills on winter's scene,
We wander forth, where dreams convene.
In this enchanted walk we find,
The splendor of the joyful mind.

Frostbitten Majesty

In the glow of winter's light,
Snowflakes dance, a sheer delight.
Joyful laughter fills the air,
Nature's beauty, beyond compare.

Trees adorned in crystal white,
Sparkle softly, pure and bright.
Children sing with hearts so free,
In this realm of jubilee.

Cups of cocoa bring us near,
Warmth spreads laughter, love, and cheer.
Together, we embrace the chill,
Moments cherished, hearts to fill.

Frostbitten land, a wondrous sight,
Wrapped in wonder, pure delight.
A festooned world, we celebrate,
In this magic, we elevate.

A Frosty Gaze

Windows glimmer, reflections play,
Twilight whispers as skies turn gray.
Eyes like stars in frosty night,
Glances warm, a sweet invite.

Candles flicker, shadows sway,
Families gather, come what may.
With every cheer and every song,
Hearts unite, where we belong.

Outside, the world's a snowy seam,
Wonders hidden in every dream.
We raise our voices, lift our mugs,
In this frosty night, we hug.

With a frosty gaze, we sip and smile,
Together we will stay awhile.
In the chill, we find our warmth,
Hope and joy, a festive storm.

Twinkles on the Tundra

Stars above a snowy field,
Whispers of the night revealed.
Glittering like diamonds bright,
Twinkles dance in pure delight.

The air is crisp, the world a balm,
Laughter echoes, everywhere calm.
Sleds are racing down the hill,
Chasing joy, we feel the thrill.

Snowmen standing guard so wide,
Waving hats, our festive pride.
With every snowball freely thrown,
We make this place forever home.

Twinkles shimmer on the ground,
In this beauty, peace is found.
Join the fun, let laughter soar,
In the tundra, we want more.

Encased in Icicles

Houses draped in shimmering frost,
A wonderland, no joy is lost.
Icicles hang like crystal slides,
Winter magic, where hope abides.

Festive lights adorn each street,
Neighbors gather with smiles to greet.
Songs of cheer float through the air,
Moments cherished, dreams to share.

Snowflakes swirl, a gentle breeze,
Warmth spreads through the frosty trees.
Mirthful whispers fill the night,
In this wonder, pure delight.

Encased in icicles, we find peace,
In this season, love will never cease.
Hearts unite in festive cheer,
Together, forever, year after year.

Splendor of the Silent Woods

Under the canopy high, stars gleam,
Whispers of joy dance on night's beam.
Branches adorned with a silver glow,
Nature's embrace, a magical show.

Laughter echoes through trees so grand,
Footprints in snow, hand in hand.
The air is crisp, the world aglow,
In this wonderland, hearts overflow.

Crystals of frost on the ground lie,
As spirits soar and dreams fly.
The silence sings a soft, sweet tune,
Beneath the glow of a radiant moon.

With every step, the magic unfolds,
In the silent woods, adventure molds.
Sipping on tales of yore and cheer,
In this splendor, joy draws near.

Reflections on Ice

A blanket of white, the earth sleeps deep,
Mirrored dreams in the ice, we keep.
Dancing lights in the frosty air,
Happiness glimmers everywhere.

Children twirl on the frozen lake,
Laughter echoes, memories they make.
As skates carve stories, young hearts race,
In this winter's wonder, we find our place.

The world transforms, everything glows,
In reflections on ice, magic flows.
Every flake that falls, a wish anew,
In this frozen land, joy breaks through.

Candles flicker, the night shines bright,
Gathered 'round warmth, hearts alight.
With friends beside and warmth inside,
In reflections on ice, we take pride.

Legends of the Frostbitten Vale

In the vale where the cool winds sigh,
Legends dance 'neath the starlit sky.
Whispers of old in the frosty air,
Tales of magic and mystery flair.

Snowflakes twist in a waltzing embrace,
Secrets of ages in every trace.
The trees stand tall, guardians of lore,
While joy spreads wide, forevermore.

Bright bonfires flicker, warmth all around,
Voices uplifted, a jubilant sound.
With spirits weaving their stories bold,
In the frostbitten vale, dreams unfold.

Footprints lead to where legends lay,
In the dance of shadows, bright as day.
Every heartbeat flows like a river's song,
In the vale of frost, we all belong.

The Whispering World of Cold

In the quiet of night where the magic swirls,
Lies the whispering world where cold unfurls.
Frosted branches play a gentle tune,
Under the gaze of a watchful moon.

Glittering crystals, a diamond's shine,
As laughter dances in lines divine.
Each breath a cloud in the chill of air,
In this world of cold, nothing can compare.

The snowflakes fall like softest sighs,
Painting the earth, a feast for eyes.
Through whispers of pine, secrets are spun,
In the heart of winter, our hearts are one.

Gather 'round, let the stories flow,
In this whispering world of frost and glow.
With every sparkle, let joy arise,
In the cold's embrace, we find our ties.

The Crystal Veil

Underneath the stars so bright,
Laughter dances through the night.
A crystal veil in moonlit glow,
Whispers secrets only we know.

Candles flicker, spirits rise,
Joyful glimmers in our eyes.
Songs of mirth fill up the air,
As friends unite, our hearts laid bare.

Delicate snowflakes, pure and white,
Drift like dreams in gentle flight.
We twirl and spin in festive cheer,
Embracing love that draws us near.

So raise a glass, let wishes flow,
In the magic of the snow.
A night adorned with dreams that sail,
Embraced within the crystal veil.

Majesty of the Shimmering Woods

In the woods where shadows play,
Glistening branches brightly sway.
Every leaf a twinkling gem,
Nature's grace, our diadem.

With a gentle, breezy sigh,
Gifts of gold from trees up high.
Whispers of the forest cheer,
Echoes of joy, loud and clear.

Gather close to share the light,
Underneath the starry night.
Candles glowing, dreams ignite,
In this majesty, pure delight.

We dance beneath the silver boughs,
A heart's glimpse, a festive vow.
Among the senses, warmth unfolds,
In the woods, where magic holds.

Winter's Heavy Heart

Beneath the weight of frosted skies,
Where winter's chill in shadows lies.
A heavy heart begins to weigh,
Yet warmth within can light the way.

Crisp air carries laughter's sound,
As friends and family gather 'round.
The hearth aglow, a comforting sight,
Spirits lifted, in the night.

Amidst the drifts of purest white,
Hope ignites with soft twilight.
In every corner, joy's embrace,
As we find warmth in this cold place.

Through winter's hold, we hold it dear,
In togetherness, we conquer fear.
For love brings light, casting aside,
The heavy heart on this festive ride.

Frosted Horizons

Frosted horizons stretch so wide,
Wrapped in blankets, nature's pride.
A sparkling quilt of white unfurls,
As magic swirls in wintry whirls.

Hot cocoa warms our chilly hands,
While snowflakes dance on frosty lands.
With laughter echoing through the trees,
We cherish moments, pure and free.

Each step leaves prints upon the ground,
In this wonderland, joy is found.
Together we create our tales,
In frosted breath and festive trails.

So let us gather, hearts entwined,
Embracing love, the purest kind.
In these horizons bright and clear,
We build a dream that we hold dear.

Nature's Winter Armor

Snowflakes dance in joyous glee,
Blanketing the world in white.
Trees wear crystals, oh so bright,
Nature's beauty, wild and free.

Children laugh, the air is pure,
Sleds rush down the sparkling hill.
Winter's magic, hearts it fills,
A season's charm, that feels so sure.

Frosty breath, the warmth of cheer,
Gathered round, we share a song.
In the glow where friends belong,
Winter's grace, we hold it dear.

Stars emerge as night draws near,
In the silence, warmth abounds.
Joy in laughter, love surrounds,
Nature's armor, crystal clear.

The Quiet Majesty of the Woods

Whispers echo through the trees,
Branches sway in gentle breeze.
Sunlight filters, soft and warm,
Nature's calm, a soothing charm.

Footsteps hush on forest floor,
Mossy carpets, tales of yore.
Leaves that shimmer, emerald hue,
A tranquil world, so fresh and new.

Birds in chorus, singing high,
Each note written in the sky.
Amidst the giants, shadows play,
The woods whisper, come what may.

Gathered here, we breathe and stand,
This sacred place, forever grand.
Nature's heartbeat, bold and true,
In every moment, life renews.

Antlers Adrift on Ice

Antlers glisten, deep in snow,
Nature's jewels set aglow.
Each fragment shines, like a dream,
Wonders caught in winter's scheme.

Reflecting light, the stillness speaks,
Beauty found in frozen peaks.
Winds whisper tales of days gone by,
Where spirits roam and shadows lie.

Crisp air bites, yet hearts feel warm,
Life holds tight through each fierce storm.
On this canvas, calm and bright,
Antlers drift in soft moonlight.

Silence reigns, the world is wide,
In this frozen realm, we bide.
Marvels hold us, heart and mind,
In nature's gift, pure joy we find.

Shivers of Solitude

Cold winds whisper through the night,
Stars cast silver, shining bright.
Lonely paths and shadows creep,
In the quiet, thoughts run deep.

Frosty whispers brush the trees,
Every breath a gentle freeze.
Silence cradle, still and wise,
In solitude, the spirit flies.

Memories dance in frosted air,
Wrapped in dreams that linger there.
The world asleep, yet I awake,
In this calm, my heart shall break.

Yet in the shiver, peace I find,
Purest moments, intertwined.
Alone, but not in bitter naught,
In solitude, I gather thought.

A Journey Through Winter's Veil.

Beneath the stars, the snowflakes dance,
Each flake a wish, a fleeting chance.
The night is bright, lanterns aglow,
As laughter rings through the crisp, cold snow.

Sleds rush by, a joyful parade,
Children's giggles in frosty cascade.
Mittens and scarves, colors so bold,
Embrace the warmth that the winter holds.

Fires crackle, stories ignite,
Bundled close, we share the night.
With cocoa sweet, hearts intertwine,
In winter's arms, we feel divine.

So here we stand, with friends around,
In this magic, our joy is found.
Life's winter journey, a splendid sight,
Together we dance in the soft moonlight.

Chilled Antlers

Amidst the pines, with snowflakes swirling,
A gentle hush, the world's unfurling.
Reindeer prance, adorned in light,
As festive echoes fill the night.

In inns aglow with laughter's cheer,
Songs of joy fill the chilly air.
With friends and family, hearts do bind,
In glowing warmth, our spirits unwind.

From rooftops high, the glittering stars,
Guide us through this night of ours.
With bells a-jingle, we wander free,
In love's embrace, we're meant to be.

Snow-white wonders, a tale so sweet,
Every step brings a heartbeat.
Together we weave this festive dream,
In chilled antlers, let our hearts beam.

Winter's Majestic Ghost

In the quiet woods, when all is still,
Winter's ghost whispers, its voice a thrill.
A blanket of white, soft like a sigh,
Cloaking the earth while stars drift by.

Branches glisten, kissed by frost,
A vivid beauty, never lost.
With every breath, the whispers call,
Let's celebrate this magic for all.

Candles flicker, a warm retreat,
Gathered close, with fires we greet.
As stories weave, time fades away,
In winter's arms, we long to stay.

And through the snow, our laughter rings,
Wrapped in joy, as the season sings.
Forever enchanted, together we rise,
In winter's embrace, beneath the skies.

The Icebound Wanderer

On frozen paths, the wanderer roams,
Under the moon, far from home.
With every step, a sparkle gleams,
In deep winter's embrace, he dreams.

Snowflakes drift like whispered tales,
Where silence reigns and magic sails.
Stars above, a guiding light,
Through icy woods, enchanting night.

Around each bend, the splendor shines,
Nature's canvas, a world divine.
With heart aglow, he strides with hope,
In winter's charm, he learns to cope.

As twinkling lights begin to glower,
He finds his place, his hour of power.
Icebound wanderer, let your spirit soar,
In the festival of warmth, forever explore.

The Silent Sentinel

In the still of night, a tree so grand,
Watches o'er the land, a steadfast stand.
Decorations twinkle, lights shine bright,
Whispers of joy fill the frosty night.

Underneath the stars, the children play,
With laughter echoing, they dance and sway.
The air is crisp, filled with festive cheer,
As the Silent Sentinel holds them dear.

Candles flicker softly, a gentle glow,
Creating warmth amidst the chill and snow.
Beneath the branches, secrets unfold,
Stories of wonder that never grow old.

Through the closing year, a spirit rings,
Hope and love are the songs that we sing.
As the moonlight bathes the world in white,
The Silent Sentinel beams with delight.

Echoes of a Snowy Vigil

Snowflakes tumble softly, a gentle fall,
Creating a blanket, a hush to it all.
Beneath the deep sky, a vigil kept,
In echoes of laughter, goodwill is swept.

Around the fire, friends gather near,
With mugs of warmth, spreading festive cheer.
Stories are woven, tales of the past,
In this snowy vigil, memories last.

The night sparkles bright with the moon's soft glow,
While shadows of joy dance on freshly laid snow.
Each flake unique, like stories to share,
In the heart of the night, we find magic in air.

As the stars twinkle high, wishes take flight,
Painting the canvas of this lovely night.
Echoes of laughter and love intertwine,
In the snowy vigil, everything's fine.

Beneath the Blanket of White

A new morning dawns, fresh and so bright,
Beneath the blanket of pure, sparkling white.
Children build snowmen, laughter abounds,
With every small snowball, joy knows no bounds.

Footprints crisscross in a festive spree,
Creating a map of blissful jubilee.
Hot cocoa awaits in the cozy retreat,
Where tales of the season are shared by the heat.

Adorned evergreen stands proud and tall,
Its branches aglow, a beacon for all.
While candles flicker, warmth fills the rooms,
Beneath the blanket, cheer brightly blooms.

As night falls again, with stars all aglow,
Families draw close, sharing warmth in the snow.
Beneath the blanket, we gather and cheer,
For love is the gift that we hold so dear.

Starlit Hooves

In the still of the night, hooves softly tread,
Carrying dreams on the path that they spread.
Under the stars, they dance and they gleam,
Whispers of magic, alive like a dream.

Festive lights twinkle, a sight to behold,
As stories of wonder and joy are retold.
Bells softly jingle, a sweet, merry sound,
In the starlit embrace, pure happiness found.

The night wraps around, a comforting cloak,
With laughter and warmth, a promise evoked.
Together we gather, in peace and in fun,
Beneath the bright sky where wishes are spun.

Starlit hooves dance on the soft, powdered ground,
Creating a rhythm, a life so profound.
In each joyful step, we celebrate cheer,
For the magic of the season draws near.